A CROWN FOR ABBA MOSES

New and Selected Poems

Timothy E. G. Bartel

Author of *Aflame But Unconsumed*

© Timothy E. G. Bartel, 2022

All rights reserved. No part of this publication may be reproduced in any form without the prior written permission of Timothy E.G. Bartel except in the case of quotations in critical reviews or other noncommercial uses permitted by copyright law.

ISBN 978-1-7359984-9-7

Cover art by Timothy E. G. Bartel, based on photograph by Clay Banks on Unsplash
Cover and interior design by Sarah Christolini

2055 E Hampton Ave, 235
Mesa, AZ 85204
(480) 371-9053
info@solumpress.com

Contents

New Poems (2019–2021)

1.

    Status Check.. 2

    Canceled.. 3

    The Old Craftsman...................................4

    St. Basil Chapel..5

    What Flesh is Heir To.............................6

    Micro-Sapphics 7

    Hymn after Harvey............................... 10

    Hymn on St. Gregory Nazianzus................12

    Another Advent....................................14

    Too Late or Not Too Late..........................16

    Autumn Elegiacs................................... 17

    Which Way I Fly.................................. 19

    The Servant of the Architect......................20

    Civics after Midnight............................22

2. A Crown for Abba Moses................................ 23

3. The Camillad.. 31

    Book One...32

    Book Two...47

    Book Three...59

Translations (2012–2021)

Major Fragments of Sappho.................................. 70

    [1].. 70

    [16].. 72

    [31].. 73

    [Brothers].. 74

    [58b].. 75

    [168b].. 76

On the Metered by St. Gregory Nazianzus...............77

Hymns of St. Ambrose... 83

    Eternal King.. 83

    Now Comes the Third Hour....................... 86

    Creator Deity.. 88

    Oh Ruler Who Guides Israel...................... 90

Epigrams of St. Kassiani......................................92

    You know what I really hate? – 12 Epigrams....92

    It's better (trust me) – 9 Epigrams.................94

Arroyos: Sijo and Other Poems (2015)

I.

    Books.. 98

    Arroyos 99
    Autumn Sijo 100
    Meditation in an English Garden 102
    Superstitions 103
    Winter Sijo 104
    Carriage: An Elegy 106

II.

    Two Nativities 109
    Belated Spring 110
    Abra, Age 8, Visits St. George's Cathedral 112
    Spring Sijo 113
    The California Condors 115
    Marriage 116
    Summer Sijo 117

The Martyr, the Grizzly, the Gold (2012)

1. Golden Sonnets 120
    Of My State 121
    The Lark 122
    The Canyon, Age 8 123
    Sillion 124
    Hardware 125
    Youth Outing 126
    Ricardo Montalban, In Memoriam 127
    Degrees 128

    Metaphors……………………………………..129

    A Baptism at Epiphany………………………130

    St Thomas's Chemistry Lesson………………131

    Spring Disjunctive…………………………... 132

2. The Martyr

    The Shaman…………………………………..134

    The Bankrupt's Prayer……………………….139

    Peter the Aleut……………………………….140

3. Exalt!

    To Moonrise…………………………………..146

    To the Mammoth……………………………... 147

    To Raindrops………………………………….148

    To Headlights…………………………………149

    To the Donut Shop……………………………150

    To Game Night………………………………..151

    To Japan………………………………………152

    To Sunset……………………………………... 153

    To the Grizzly………………………………...154

    On the Road…………………………………... 155

    To the Reader, from the Hermit……………… 156

    The Gold……………………………………...157

    Of My State, 2………………………………... 158

Four Counties (2011)

1. Ventura...160
2. Los Angeles.. 161
3. Riverside..163
4. San Luis Ob5spo.......................................165

New Poems

(2019–2021)

1.

Which way I fly is Hell, myself am Hell

    —*Paradise Lost* 4.75

    I hear

My ill-spirit sob in each blood cell,

as if my hand were at its throat. . . .

I myself am hell;

nobody's here—

    —Robert Lowell, "Skunk Hour," ll. 32–36

We hear too late or not too late.

    —Geoffrey Hill, "Christmas Tress," l. 9

Status Check

Try to make sense of what happened when you were alive:
Where was there justice? How hot were the breezes in August?
Where were the altars? To whom was the sacrifice offered?
Who were the men you were punished for slandering? Which songs
Played at the feasts and the weddings? and who was forbidden to sing
    them?

Canceled

Who is it watching you from nearby eyes
Who notes repeated phrases and distinctions
You make throughout your study and your play?
Who is it that records your conversations
If not on tape, at least in memory,
And practices your speeches as their own?
You fear it is the critics, ready to
Accuse you of your cruel or thoughtless terms.

But fear far more the one who is in earnest
And makes of you a pattern for their art
Of living, judging each internal shift
Of their own thoughts by your external acts.
For you remember how your idols died:
At first in estimation, then indeed.

The Old Craftsman

The brief asphyxiations peak at dawn.
He whittles down his plans and arguments
Again against the lack of time, the known
Despised uncertainty of each next day.
But still he toys with anxious wishes for
Another fame or one last masterpiece.
His wishes rise, and grope, and settle as
His final breath inscapes, escapes.
                                          Yes, this,
My soul, is how the next old craftsman dies,
The next, the next. A queue of dying forms
Is set that will arrive, at last, at you.
What will your little toils at making seem
When breath itself becomes a rationed thing?
Be wary with what arrogance you sing.

St. Basil Chapel

–University of St. Thomas, Spring 2020

The emptiness of Houston is acute,
As empty as the bayou shores where once
The native fishermen caught native fish
And not one face of Houston's race had seen
Their own reflection in the browning stream.
The space where there had been a level plain
Is gouged at angles only men could make.

There is an empty place within this wall,
A cross-shaped void; above it He is stretched
In some creative feat of hovering.
The cross will never cease to be a cross.
It cannot be back-filled; that's not His way.
The only sure direction we can take
Is forward, through the empty, toward His arms.

What Flesh is Heir To

There was once asphalt here, but now new grass
Growing in tufted rectangles of sod,
Their little roots reintroducing soil,
So long kept dormant, to a life again.
The water from a recent rain makes mud
At every edge where sod meets sod; my feet
Attempt to step where there is only green.
I fear my clumsy walking will dislodge
The little permanence it has achieved.

I've mourned to see the parking lots expand,
And smother soil to sleep, to wake no more.
But here before me is a little plot
Reversing, root by root, the larger trend.
I know it's not so radical or grand,
But brother, let us love the thing we have.

Micro-Sapphics

1.

Spring is a warning,

warming the Gulf with

    wind and cloud-bank.

2.

Into the thunder

freeways redent like

    glyph-less temples.

3. *The Teacher*

Form me a morning

brimming with coffee

    and a classroom.

4.

Lyric as lime bite,

lip from a fist fight,

        split by primed sight.

5. *The Piano*

White in the dusking

light of the storm-fringe:

        fifty-two keys.

6. *The Iconographer*

Lightly he washes

ceilings in sea blue,

        then the gold stars.

7.

April is ending—

even the concrete

      pipe sprouts flowers.

8.

Past the enchantment
history wrecks is
      resurrection.

Hymn after Harvey

The storm first taught my oak tree how

To shatter, branch by brittle branch,

To crackle like a snare drum roll

Each time a bough would stagger down.

It left a stump to still remove,

A hunkered place immune to storm,

So I am trying out the thought

That flame will root what water can't.

I heat up coals as if to grill,

But when they're white, I tong them in

To grooves and fissures in the stump,

Then wait for brown to turn to black,

And watch the smoke catch currents of

September wind behind my house

Beneath a sky still traumatized

From kettle drums of numbing rain:

The rain that scaled the bayous, filled

The streets, the sidewalks, and the yards,

Then slipped, unbidden, into rooms,

And pulped the foam inside the walls.

I, too, was there to rip it out:

My neighbor's insulation with

The drywall in his flooded house.

I scraped a playing card from where

It clung onto his tile, beside

His daughter's plastic high-heeled shoes,

Two rusting pocket mirrors, and

A warped blue book of Faerie Tales.

And now that these are in your mind,

Don't add them yet to curbside trash,

But hold them hard within yourself

Between your wisdom and your fear.

Hymn on St. Gregory Nazianzus

    c. 330–390 AD

At midnight you were once aroused
By two bright women at your bed
Who named themselves as Chastity
And Virtue. And they asked to live

Within your young and striving heart.
I think of Basil, who you loved,
Who so offended your ideals
Of friendship and of brotherhood;

And even so, you spoke before
His grave and told the weeping crowd:
*His words were thunder, for his life
Was like the lightning.* What would men

Give for a gift of words like yours?
How many would say *No* to those
Bright offices they offered you:
Chief orator, Archbishop? Woe

They were to you, those titles most
Desire. Shepherd of my mind,
You seem most happy writing out
Your rural letters in old age:

You count dactylic lines and smile,
So glad you gave up speech for Lent.
It's best to pour what force remains
In us into some careful craft,

Then seal it up, and send it to
An unsuspecting friend who will
On reading it discover our
Complexities of meter mean *I love you*.

Another Advent

The moon is waxing, on the verge

Of mid-fall full. The stars are sharp:

Orion's belt stands out behind

Thin cloud, a mist like Milky Way

But closer. The whole heaven seems

To bend toward earth tonight. All stars

Are local stars, and if you stand

Just right the moon seems straining at

A frame of oak-boughs. When I hear

The yawn of passing freeway cars

I think of them as headed toward

Some far off point, and this quick town

Must seem to them as foreign as

The last, and yet it feels like home

To me, and I am comforted

By this, by other travelers:

The vanishing sedan, the train,

The stars themselves that slowly go

Past place, past time, past very self,

Imploding, nova-sapped, into

A passageway for light and mass

To disappear into at last,

And end up who knows where—perhaps

A little corner village in

Some distant galaxy, where oaks

Are young, and leaves are falling still,

And shuffling fathers stoop to rake

Them from the gutters, for it looks

Like rain may come tonight; if not,

Perhaps tomorrow, as the month

Revolves again toward Christmas when

The timeless for the first time felt time's weight.

Too late or not too late

There comes a sense as Fall is lengthening
That you are too far in to draw your mind
Back out to summer, or to what you thought
In spring. The leaves are much too brown, and in
The mornings there is frost as often as
There's not. You're made complicit with the year,
With its accomplishments and with its guilt,
With all the things concluded in its span:

A book that's finally read, the argument
That never got resolved, a failure to
Explain yourself to those who were confused.
I'd like to say: it's not too late for you—
There is no snow upon the roads just yet;
There's light to still repent and not forget.

Autumn Elegiacs

    1.

Cultivate in you the habit of seasons: be patient with days and with
    minutes;
    Think of the planning it takes to redouble the effort:
Somewhere the universe chooses to enter the winter again—what
    Courage resides in cosmos, made strong by the memory
Ever of leaf-fall, then of the bare boughs, then of the pink buds.

    2.

Hundreds of thousands of light years away are the forges of new stars,
    Churning their mass flame out to the dark of the cosmos,
Out to the shores of this planet, this Earth where I look into your eyes.

    3.

It is December again, and the air is as warm as it was when
    We were expecting October to grow cool. Say it's
True, and the warm will indeed become hot; cool warm, and the cold just
    Ceases to be on the earth, and that somewhere the snow will
Fall for the last time, last hold all of its freezing in soil,
    Coax every dewdrop to harden a last time,
Saying: goodbye to the earth, goodbye from the aeon of glaciers.
    Still it will stay on the poles for while, but then gone.
How many humans will live on this Earth then? Only a few? Will
    All turn colonist, shaping with boot-soles the soil of

New Mars, looking up into the sky, and discerning, past sunset,
    Glow from an alien earth in the saddening star-scape?

    4.

Come to an ending again, the eternal return to a resting:
    How does the poetry close? With a couplet or spondee
That is surprising and fit, that reconciles images prior, which
    Seemed on the outset irrelevant—they're now shown to be
Tied at a level profound, where the words disappear into image, and
    All we are left with is visceral senses imagining;
That is the way to go out, though in history, wracked with particulars,
    Go in the way that engages the mind in its making,
Leaving your audience reeling, as Pound did with wet, black boughs once.

Which way I fly

What is the meaning of the sunlight on
The wooden floor, the long reflected lines
Of shine and shade where each board joins the next?
It means the worry of a long disease,
Where every room reminds of the routine
You fear to lose and fear to still perform;
Or does it mean the kindness of a sun
That feels already in its massive dance
The coming final steps and stumblings that
Will plunge the floorboards, cities, planets in
A darkness near impossible to light
Unless the human spirit can be healed?
For history's a slow disease as well,
As Lowell saw when he himself was hell.

The Servant of the Architect

> – Frank Lloyd Wright's Taliesin House, WI.
> August 15, 1914.
> Seven dead, including murderer.

Though born in Trinidad I serve
The master now in winter halls
Beside his hearths of ruddy brick,
In cramped domestic quarters. His

Too famous forms have morphed of late;
These days he builds with concrete blocks
Inlaid with flowers, mountains, wheat
Abstracted till they're crystalline.

He's modernized the structures of
The rich man's life, made open air
The costliest of walls. No more
For him the cordoned parlor and

No more the heavy doors; let space
Blend into every other space;
Drape rivers through the living rooms;
Let sky itself replace the roof.

He's gone tonight, to work or flirt,
And I have gathered here some rough
Materials: wood, steel, grudge, flame,
To play ironic architect:

This axe's blade, for instance, slides
So smooth between his lover's ribs;
This fire seems invented to
Absolve his bedposts of their stain,

And has a belly big enough
To hold his living-room and still
Be hungry for the shadows in
His halls. The only paint I have

Is what is boiling from the necks
Of these black bodies. Did I dream
Or did I read that red was once
The costliest of colors? Please

Bear with me. I am construct too
And open up so easily.
My act of art will enter his—
I will dissolve with all his walls.

Civics after Midnight

Imagination is a monarchy;

They cannot rule where they cannot decree.

Just think of Solzhenitsyn underground,

His manuscripts in danger, not his mind.

Trust not in princes is for poets too;

To order what's within is up to you.

They'll never rule where they cannot decree —

Imagination is a monarchy.

2.

A Crown for Abba Moses

c. 330–405 AD

1.

When Moses had escaped from slavery
(Many years before he was called Abba)
He settled on the best course for his life:
To be a thief and lead a crew of thieves,
"To teach the sons of bitches 'cross the Nile
The lesson that we learned while still inside:
The longest lasting memories you make
Are scars you carve into your enemy."

They sought him in Egyptian caves: the cons,
The lads intent on sex and coin, the slaves
Who sickened of their masters and so slit
Their greasy gullets on a summer night.
The name of Moses echoed down the Nile:
He'll snuff a snitch, or steal your wife for fun.

2.

This hustler called Big Xerxes had three rams
He'd brag about. He'd spit at Moses as
He passed him on the street; he'd flash his gold,
And wager it, and win. Well, Moses got
Piss-drunk enough one night to pay him back.
He left his crew carousing in the hills
And swam across the Nile to Xerxes' farm,
A knife, a forearm long, gripped in his teeth.

But as he was about to step inside
The house, a dog leaped up within the doorway
And almost caught his windpipe in its jaws.
Undaunted, Moses left the house alone.
Instead he found Big Xerxes' boasted rams
And ate their butchered chops beneath the moon.

3.

It was a hell of hiding places, that
Raw, earth-roofed desert chapel that he could
Have ripped the walls off. Cops from Cairo paced
Around the chapel several times, described
The suspect to the monks: "A big guy, Black.
The kind you hear about in town, who'll steal
Your daughter day before her wedding, leave
Her bruised and knocked-up in a ditch somewhere."

The monks all shook their heads and looked confused,
A few were Black as he, but thin, as if
They never ate enough. He ate their bread,
But shrugged away their invitations to
Come into church. He stuck around a week,
A month, a winter. Then, he tried to pray.

4.

He came to Abbot Isodore one day,
And said: "My father, I have learned to pray
My daily rule now to the point that I
Have come to like it, but more strong than that
Are my desires for women: every night
I strap my sandals on and head down to
The whorehouse, buy a woman, climb in bed,
Then wake up in my cell unsatisfied:
How can a man with so much passion not
Give in and have his way?" The elder took
Young Moses to a tower's top and said:
"Look West": and there were swarms of demons, clogged
In every desert cave. "Look East": and there
Were twice as many angels, strapped for war.

5.

A monk was caught in petty lies and lust
And so the monastery priest had called
A meeting in the church so each could chide
The wayward one. But Moses would not come.
The priest insisted on his presence there,
But Moses still delayed. Impatient, all
Marched out to find him at his cell. Toward them
He limped beneath a ragged sack of sand
Which slopped behind him by the bucketful.
He sighed: "My brothers, see this bag of sand?
It holds my many sins. They pour behind
Me, but I cannot see them, for I come
To judge my brother and ignore myself."
And so they each forgave the wayward monk.

6.

The four thieves found him at his evening prayers:
"He's middle-aged;" "His knees look weak;" "A quick
And easy score;" "His altar looks like gold."
Two pulled their shivs and flanked him, two moved toward
The loot. His leg swept like an iron broom.
They dropped, their ankles numb. He hulked erect
And whipped his blanket round their aching heads,
Then carried them, all bruised and bundled up
Into the chapel, dropped them on the stone.
They recognized him: "Moses!" "Isn't he
The one that laid the Pharaoh's daughter?" "He
Burned Aphra's farm." They waited for his knife.
But Moses said: "A Christian does not kill."
They gaped. Then bowed. Then asked him how to pray.

7.

One morning Abba Moses said: "They come,
A host of thieves, fulfilling what Christ said:
That those who live by blades will die by them."
The brothers swore to stay with him, but he
Persuaded all but seven monks to flee.
They waited till the dust of hooves was close,
Then filled the chapel: sunset filtered down
And lit each forehead like a laurel crown.
Then Abba Moses felt a pang of lust
For one more girl before the end. He smiled
At his exhausted passions' final try.
Next came a fear of pain. This too he mocked.
He'd readied to be murdered all his life—
Then blade-glare—then escape from slavery.

3.

THE CAMILLAD

I saw Camilla and Penthesilea
On the other side, and saw the King Latinus,
Who with Lavinia his daughter sat.
        Inferno IV.124–126

BOOK ONE

A well-waged war was once a woman's work.
Camilla, daughter of an exiled king
And wife to no man chose that battle-task
When queens around her foundered in their ends.
And I request that you, my reader, in
Your modern mind now tune these lines to sing
Camilla's war-work and her end. Begin,
Attentive muse, on that auspicious day
Camilla stood before Lavinia
And sought the council of the Latin princess.

In Latium, where King Latinus reigned,
Within the white-walled castle of the King,
The princess sat in tension, caught between
Two rival suits of princes: Turnus, first—
By blood and by alliance he had claim
And local right to wed her and to draw
The Latins and Ritullians into
A lasting friendship based on blended thrones.
But from the East another suitor rose:
Aeneas, son of Venus, prince of Troy;
To him the prophets said high Jupiter
Had promised all the land of Latium
And his descents after him until

His grandson's grandsons, nursed by wolves, would lift
The walls of Rome that time could hardly raze.

Lavinia, beleaguered by these suits,
Had hidden, waiting in her father's courts
To hear reports from war outside those walls
Where Turnus and Aeneas hurled their men
Against each other, hoping battle would
Decide her husband and the fate of Rome.
But now before her came another of
Her age and sex; instead of lace she wore
A leather doublet, copper breastplate, spear
Of knotted myrtle like a shepherd's staff,
But tipped in iron for the death of men.

"I come as ally from the Volscians,"
Camilla said, and bowed as men will bow
Before exacting generals or kings.
"The royal Turnus has accepted my
Request to serve as cavalry in his
Attempt tomorrow on the Trojan lines."
Lavinia, amused and curious
Asked: "Why, if Turnus is your ally do
You come before me, acting, as I sense,
As if you need permission from myself?

For Turnus is commander of the troops
Of Latins and Ritullians, and I
Am little better than a captive here,
Unable to go out because of battle,
Unable to be calm because of worry,
Unable to give comfort to the king,
My father, who has shut himself away,
In anger and confusion at the war
That's waged before his gates without consent
Of him who rules the gates. I have no strength
To give permissions or rescind them now.
I am a thing distilled into a milk
Of patience, hoping for single wedding
To end this war, and not two funerals."

"I do not come," Camilla answered her,
"To ask permission, but instead your will.
I also am a thing distilled. Since birth
My father trained me in the arts of war.
For while I was an infant, civil strife
Arose in Volsci, drove my father to
Abandon—sore but sure—his rightful throne
His royal armor, and his luxuries,
And flee with me into the wilderness
Escaping from the mobs that marched to burn
His golden palace and our holy shrines.

His enemies had found our route, and came
Upon us in the wilderness where we
Were backed up to a river's bank; it held
Black water and black night and blacker death.
The journey to the blackest underworld
Seemed certain, when my father through his fear
Discovered his defiance and his faith.
For there he prayed: 'Diana, goddess of
The hunt, and virgin patron of these glades,
I call upon you now to guide my spear
Across this river, deep as sleep. The child
I bind unto this shaft I bind as well
Unto your virgin service if you save
Her life and guide her to the further shore!'
He tied me in a bundle to the shaft,
And kissed with tenderness my little fists
In blessing. Then he hurled me out of reach
Of those oncoming enemies. I soared
Like Jove's own eagles soar above the Alps,
Above the Amazonian waters, past
Their further bank, and landed on the soil
That I would call my home for many years.
He swam across then, hoping with each stroke
To find me on the shore and not in depths
Untouched by time. At last he saw my face
Alive with smiles and safely on the land.

Behind me stood the woodlands and the hills
Where sheep and wolves and feral tigers roam,
Contending for their lives among the wilds
Which Jove's own daughter calls her earthly home.
My father swore forever to renounce
His royal claim and seek a simple life
As shepherd and as tutor to myself,
My tutor in the arts of hunt and arms
And all the strengths of women sacred to
Diana, who retains her virgin might.
He taught my feet to run as swiftly as
The wind across the Adriatic waves;
I learned the sweat of labor in the close
And shadowed trees, the thrill of hunting blind
At midnight where the scent of tiger's breath
Brought me so near the jaws of death that I
Could smell the drying flowers on the crown
Of Hecate herself; but drawing back
From her eternal arms, I plunged my blade
And made the beast that would have killed me mine
For warmth in winter and a coat of glory."
And as she heard these words, Lavinia
Became aware Camilla wore striped furs
Around her shoulders—yes, indeed it was
A coat of glory, and the princess saw
In her imagination those dark woods,

That wild tiger gushing out his life
And stout above him, glistening in triumph
The armed Camilla, heir of Amazons.

Camilla searched Lavinia for some
True indication of her will, and said:
"I say these things to give assurance of
My might, my chance of turning this whole war
To my own will, if only for a time. And so I ask:
What is your will, my princess? Turnus chose
To let me lead the cavalry, so he
Might win your hand. But what is your own will?
If I withhold my might, I can allow
Aeneas' spear to pierce Prince Turnus' breast
And gain you Trojan offspring for all time.
Or I can ride, and in my riding loose
The power of Diana to the cause
Of local Turnus. My conclusion is:
I have a work of war to do before
I greet the goddess Hecate below,
And I will spend it in the aid of those
Who need it most. And so: what is your will?"

Then in Camilla's eyes Lavinia
Discerned a woman unafraid to die
Unwed, and having given birth to none,

And unregretful of these things, which seemed
A loss—perhaps the greatest loss—to her.
"And do you truly mean that you will choose
The life of arms instead of that of wife?
Or were you scorned in love, which made you seek
A final death in glory on the field?"

Camilla answered, "When I came of age,
And I displayed the womanhood that men
All crave to see, and hold, and call their own,
My father entertained a dozen suits
And more from local noblemen and knights.
But I would choose not one among them all,
And though my father begged me to repent
In front of each young man who came to call,
When I refused and they had sulked away,
Then he would praise me, lead me to the glens
That held Diana's altars; we would light
The votive flames together, thanking her,
Diana, for the gifts she gives to girls—
And chief of these, virginity: the life
That, undistracted, can pursue the hunt,
Preserve the hand for only grasping spears,
And never shackled to the wedding ring.

"I did once wonder, deep within the woods,
If I had chosen rightly, for I had
Pursued a stag for days, and, weary with
Hard hunting, thirsting for a stream, I cried
Into the shadowed woods: 'What is this life?
A lonely one of waiting, for the chase
Will never find reward nor will achieve
A work of victory to match the years
I spent in training in these wasted woods!'
I heard in answer to my echoed cries
A far, faint song, as of a girl, or stream.
I searched to find the source of song, footsore,
Arms black with dust except where streaked with sweat.
As I drew back a leaf-thick olive bough,
I saw the sight that none have seen and lived:
The virgin goddess, bright and bathing in
A pool of perfect water. Perfect form
Inhered in every limb and living breath,
And how her skin shone did not hide her, but
Revealed each inch of her more sharp than life,
As if the sun had never lit the world
Until it shone on her: her brow, her deep
Black hair… I cannot tell you further, for
Description would fall short and would arouse
In any mortal mind impious thoughts.
But on that day I looked on her and lived.

"I noticed, shying eyes away from her,

That all around her sat her singing nymphs:

Each wore an armor never seen on Earth,

Their adamants of green, and black, and orange

Like summer sunset. One of them, I saw

With shock, was looking straight at me, and held

A golden bow bent back so far its tips

Were touching one another, yet she held

It almost casually as if amused

At me, and curious what I would do.

Diana looked at her, then looked along

Her eyebeams toward me, and the goddess' eyes,

In seeing me, were soft. She beckoned with

Her fingers, each so dextrous-graceful that

I seemed to be the bowstring pulled by them.

'Oh Oris, vigilant, put down your bow,

And let my suppliant approach my pool,'

She said, and I was wading in, and I

Unclasped my tunic, dropped my bow, as if

It were the proper thing to be unclothed

There in the gaze of she who drew my gaze.

"I now remember that I heaved with sobs,

As I was wading out to her, but then

It seemed that I was happier than words,
And could not cry while looking on her face.
I stood before her, lank, and smudged, and bare,
My copper skin, compared to hers, a shade.
She smiled and took a deep, low breath, and—what
Was I beholding? For it seemed to me
The surface of the pool itself rose up
Into a cloud. Diana waved her hand
Across my shoulders, then my breasts, then waist,
And I was clothed again in living mist.
'Though you may see me, child, I give this dress
To you to hide you from all other eyes.'
And then she stooped and raised two hands like cups
Of brimming water, and she washed my arms,
My forehead, and my feet; and at her touch
I felt the years of weary training change
And sweeten into surety and strength.

"At last she pressed my breastbone with her palm.
At first I felt as if a blade had pierced
My chest, but that soon passed. Replacing it,
A thundering rang through my shivered frame
As if the hooves of every deer pursued
By every hunter bounded through my bones.
And now I felt my skin from neck to thighs
En-traced by sharp, thin rivulets of cold

As if a hundred rivers crossed my form.
I looked down at the cloud around me and
It seemed to all be moving: mounting high
And dark in places, and in ragged strands
In others, till I saw before me not
The body of a girl, but that of Earth.
Then over me the winter passed: the rain
Of continents was cool upon my back
Until it was a pool and then a stream
That wound around my waist and found the sea
That bloomed between my ribs. And deeper in,
I felt my bones like earthquakes shift and ache,
As if there were a restlessness below,
A molten hunger at the core of me.

"I was the Earth while high Diana held
My self transformed within in her hand, and I
Experienced a spring, I think, at last:
For every sinew, every pore was filled
With that deep hunger till I felt I could
No longer hold it in, and I let forth
A cry that was not cry, but rather life:
I was a bud becoming leaves and vines,
And trees which aged millennia while I
Was gasping from the suddenness and still
I saw myself becoming every grove,

And every forest that there ever was
Or will be, and I saw within each grove
An altar to Diana, and a pool
In which two stood, a goddess and a girl.
And looking at the girl, I found myself.
Then I was standing in a little stream
Alone, and I was clad as usual,
Except my arms and feet were clean, and I
No longer feared I'd lead a wasted life."

Amazed at her, Lavinia replied:
"Though so devoted to Diana's aims,
And blessed by her with surety of your call
You still would fight to win for me a husband
Though you will never take one for your own?"
Camilla, filled with confidence replied:
"Diana guides her servants to assist
Each woman who is forced to choose against
A life that wakes the deepest work in her—
And you are such a woman. Here I stand
And seek from you a battle where I may
Express the gift Diana gave me for
The scrum and strife. When I have died or won
I hope to be convinced that it was worth
The height of art I plan to exercise.
I do not know why some have chosen to

Devote themselves to Venus or to Juno.
They seem to me the gods of other girls,
But if a devotee of them could need
My arrows of Diana in her aid,
I could, I think, serve Jupiter's high wife
By serving well his daughter in the fray."

"In present war," Lavinia explained,
"I fear that Juno is in conflict with
Aeneas—for, if prophets speak the truth,
He is the son of Venus, and the one
Who wins his hand will be enraptured by
That goddess who brings deepest sweetness to
The living, sweetness that will last past death
And be the memory we treasure when
All light has left, and we are only shades.
But I am torn by this, for Turnus is
A man beloved of Juno, who is fierce
In war against her enemies as she
Is kind in blessing wives who marry well."

"If you are torn," Camilla said, "then choose
To favor neither with your choice. You could
Join me, and fight with me—for I have drawn
A host of women to my virgin cause,

And in the coming fight their arrows will

Pierce throats, pin limbs, spark fear in hearts of men."

"I have no arms for fighting, nor a heart.

I want the wedding and the family

That Juno gives and blesses—but which man?

I have known Turnus since my youth and think

Him strong and proud like men in ancient tales

Who wed a wife and kill a king and give

New laws to lawless peoples. I do not

Know this Aeneas; I have seen him, seen

A weariness within his eyes, but fire

To find a home and rest from wandering.

Too many of my sisters were informed

Who they would wed, and when, and had no say.

But I have seen in you a woman who

Would have her choice though all may stand against

Her will. If I could do the same, I would.

I will attempt a choice then: fight for me.

Assume the leadership of cavalry

Beside prince Turnus. Let the war decide,

But war with woman's element within.

They say that Penthesilea was there

Within the Trojan ranks before the end

Of all the Trojan race. Why should my war

Be less than that of Helen? I would have

An Amazon upon the bloody plain."

A satisfaction filled Camilla's eyes,
As if the war she sought to wage appeared
To her a poem stressed with victories.
But fear arose within Lavinia—
She saw she was condemning this brave girl
To death, perhaps, regardless of which man
Would win. For woman's place, she thought at last,
Was not in arms upon the field, but in
Some place apart from men, where neither wars
Of men nor suits of men could swerve
Them from their chosen daily tasks: the loom,
The lyre, the planting, and the harvesting.
Or else, if men could be redeemed from war
And warlike wooing, then a woman may
Accept them so redeemed. All this she thought
As pleased Camilla left, but did not say.

BOOK TWO

Diana has attended to this pact
Of potent women from her mountain throne,
And Oris is awaiting her command.
They watch Camilla passing through the streets
Of Latium. They see the women peek
Out from their windows, at their wash or meal,
And little daughters gaze at her with awe
To see a woman draped in tiger skin,
In golden armor, with a leather strap
Around her forehead like a ready sling
To turn from crown to weapon in a flash.
The little ones pretend they swing that sling,
And older women wonder what a sword
Would feel like in their flour-covered hands;
Their eyes stray to a broomstick or a staff
They use for walking, and they see a spear.

The virgin goddess sighs to see them dream:
"What can I do in this late age where men
Forget the virgin huntress, leave my shrines
Untended, piling all their votaries
On Mars' red altars, overflowing with
The pleas of men for male victory?
Where are my Amazons, whose deeds of old

Have balanced out the ages with their strength?
Where is my Penthesilea, who with
Her cavalry of Amazons once made
The Greeks themselves feel freezing fear? Where is
The queen Hippolyta who dared to shame
Great Hercules himself for hubris? All
Are dead in myths long past, or buried in
The Trojan ground, now trampled with Greek jeers.
And where are those they left? They are dispersed
And sail wide, to lands unseen by eyes
Of mortal women—strong Gertrida passed
Beyond the sight of history to wait
Till later ages to display her strength.
Who champions my causes now? I see
Just one: Camilla, brandishing a spear
That would be better held by shepherd's hands
To hurl back the wolves from precious flocks.
Go, Oris, bring her fitter weapons from
Our own Olympian armories: an axe,
A quiver full of sharp, light javelins,
New bow and arrows, and a shield that tells
The story of the gloried Amazons."

Nymph Oris, quick as arrows fly, departs,
And, gathering the weapons, whirls down
To earth to find Camilla calling all

Her girls, her cavalry, to arms. Here is
Tarpeia twirling axes, ready to
Rend heads; here is Larina, Tulla, and
Dear Acca, who rides always at the side
Of her Camilla, brandishing a lance.
The girls marvel at the nymph's appearance,
And wind sweeps round their meeting. Oris gives
Camilla first the axe, its handle wrapped
In shining leather straps; its heavy head
Is sharpened adamantine that can cut
Through bone like butter and through iron too.
And next she gives the quiver full of darts:
Their shafts are light and smooth, their heads
Are adamantine like their sister axe;
And next the bow with golden limbs to match
The one that Oris has for slaying foes.
See finally the shield she gives Camilla:
It's round and copper, spiraled with reliefs
That hold the history of Amazons:
For here Hippolyta is dealing with
Great Hercules who suffered through twelve trials
In penance for the murder of his wife.
Hippolyta is hearing his request:
That she give up her war-belt so he may
Deliver it unto to king of Tyrins
To whom he is in debt. The pinnacles

Of Themiscyra frame the famous scene,

Where queen Hyppolita considers well

The troubled man's request—but back behind

The queen, sly Hera, queen of gods, has stirred

The Amazons with battle wrath, and they

Are ready to advance upon the man

Who dares to strip their monarch of her belt.

Beside this scene another runs: this time

Antiope accepts abduction by

The subtle Theseus, who called himself

A hero, but who poets call a cad.

For see, he pulls Antiope away

From lands she knows to Athens, while she turns

Still half in love with Themiscyra, home,

But half-enamored with the love of this

Impressive warrior, though he is a man.

But next, behold the outcome of this theft:

Athens in flames, and Amazons who hold

The upper heights of Aereopagus

Against the men of Theseus who know

Too little of how wars are waged on hills

Amid the changing levels of the rocks.

They now despair their city has been lost

To those invading Amazons who struck

With fury for their lost Antiope.

See Penthesilea next, who rode to aid

The Trojans in their war against the Greeks.
She gallops toward Achilles, leaving piles
Of Argives in her wake. Achilles does
Not know the grief that he will meet when she
Is dying in his arms, his spear lodged in
Her now-beloved chest, nor that he will
Afford her body honors he withheld
From even Hector in his famous wrath.
And finally, a future scene plays out,
To make the cycle of engraving whole:
Here brave Lucretia turns a sword against
Herself to prove her testament to men
Too stubborn to believe her self-report
That Tarquin, tyrannous, has ravaged her.
For see, Lucretia slays herself, her sword
Is piercing through her breastbone as the men
Of Rome, the senators, all blanch from shock
And pledge revenge upon the Tarquins now.
Camilla straps her arm with all these tales
And mounts her waiting steed, a gray-blue mare
Whose mother was her father's and whose milk
Once whet Camilla's lips when she was young
And had no living mother, save that mare.

Now populate a field with armies, see
Camilla's lines of cavalry along

the walls, and, facing them across the field,
The lines of Trojan horsemen and behind
A grove. Imagine that those trees are just
Fog-daubed enough in shadow you could think
Them deep and full of mystery, but still
Not of such interest you forget the field.
The grass from far appears a furring green
That lines of horses muddle with hard hooves.
Like statues see the war-ranks posed,
The sweat on women's faces poised to drip,
Sweat running down opposing brows of men
Already—and beyond the men those woods.
Distract yourself a little with them, think
Of trunks receding: sharp, then dull, then gone
Into a darkness goddesses could fill.
(Oh, this is all imagined, but believe
It still—a diorama of a world
You peek into and thrill to still achieve
Belief in all the details of its craft.
Though you are not a child you still desire
To find a fantasy within this world.)

Now tall upon her steed Camilla sees
Aeneas' cavalry approaching toward
The walls of Latium, and at their head
Etruscan Arruns, from whose loins the line

Of Tarquin will descend and ruin thrones.

Camilla leads her cavalry to meet them;

Her girls' lance-tips form a grove of steel.

They cross the line of danger—arrow range.

The Trojan javelins and arrows rise

And carve their slow and deadly arcs, but these

Horse-maidens, dexterous, have been trained to track

And doge the lazy arrow in the sky,

To even catch descending javelins

And hurl them back at he who threw them first.

And so, between the closing lines of horses,

A dark exchange is raging—arrows, darts,

And now the lances tilt and couch on hips.

The chargers meet: Camilla's myrtle lance

Surprises Arruns' horse and strikes the strap

That keeps his saddle on: he topples off,

And curses at this unmanned girl, who turns

To check her cavalry, who are retreating.

Two times she rallies them to clash with Trojans.

Two times they're beaten back with force; so far

They almost feel the walls of Latium

Against their backs. But they are led by one

Who lends tenacity to every girl.

The third advance to keep the Trojans back

Dissolves into a free-for-all: here one

Etruscan fights a Volscian, here two

Tenacious Trojans chase a fleeing rider.
But where the fray is thickest, she is found:
Camilla, daughter of the wily King,
The nursling of the wild mare, the one
Still-mortal woman who has looked upon
Diana in her glory and remained
Among the living. Hers was work and play
And pleasure and instruction all in one.
The first she challenges is Eunaeus;
He's slow to notice how she reaches in
Her quiver and removes a javelin—
Long, light, and ripe for throwing. In his chest
She lodges it. He drops, still fumbling for
His useless sword. She whirls her mare around
As quickly as tornadoes change their course;
She catches Liris, too, unready for
The lunge of lance she plunges in his side,
Then rips back out, and with it brings a gush
Of Trojan blood that once dyed Phrygia.
And Pagasus, the namesake of the steed
Of Hercules, attempts to catch his friend,
The dying Liris, but quick Acca drives
Her spear between them, letting Liris fall
To Latin dust. She lays his friend beside him
With one quick flick of spear-point 'cross his throat.

The Trojans start to give Camilla berth;
They ride in wider circles from her rage,
And further from the Latin gate, their goal.
But they misjudge her arm, begin to act
As targets for her javelins' precision.
Amaster thinks he's far enough away
And watches as she lofts her dart high out
Across the morning sky; he sees it tip
Down toward him, but cannot believe its range
Until it strikes him down below the brow
And shatters in his skull just at the nose.
As Chromis laughs to see the Trojan fall
And blesses his Etruscan sense, he feels
A scalding pain as Tulla's arrow cuts
Into his neck. He offers all his blood,
Then, to the ground. Another follows him,
Harpalycus, who dodged the Argive blades
When Troy was sacked, but cannot dodge the gash
Camilla's javelin has given him.

Two die, then five, then ten, then Trojan men
Despair of ever reaching those high walls
From which the Latin women look amazed
To see Camilla's bright, unwearied arms
Pluck from Diana's quiver one more dart
And send it through the chest of Ornytus.

She cries to him: "You thought you were immune
By riding careful, further back than those
Who fell before you. Know that this whole plain
Belongs to me! My arms can gather all
Who step their feet on it, and introduce
Them to the blade that ends their male life.
Perhaps you should beseech the gods to place
Your soul into a woman's body next
So that you might in time ally with girls
Who keep you from the walls so easily!"
But dim Ornytus does not hear this last
Exulting taunt: he is already shade,
And rather than Camilla's voice he hears
The whispering of deathly Hecate.

Orchylicus, Ornytus' kin, has heard
Enough brash taunting from this Amazon-
So-called. He spurs his horse to charge. And as
Camilla reaches down to grab one more
Sharp javelin to halt him fast, she finds
The quiver empty. Smiling, she sits up,
And as he reaches her, she leaps away,
Her mare delighted at the chance of chase.
Camilla rides in circles: now she's close
To Trojan lines who wince before her glance,
And now she's near the Latin walls. Her turns

Grow tighter, tighter, till the whirling chase

Seems almost up to proud Orchylicus.

But as Camilla seems to lean too far,

To dodge her foe's first spear thrust, she springs up,

And standing full upon her mare's wide back

She plunges down her patient axe upon

The terrified Orchylicus' raised arms

And hacks away until they are mere stumps.

Then with a final slash across his face

She cuts in half his final, pleading wheeze.

But as she settles back from brutal work,

She sees another Trojan has approached

The wall, and others follow him. Her mare,

Unwearied by her circling game, beats all

And wheels between the gate and charging men.

The Trojan leader at their head calls out:

"Your mare is fine, and so far helps you hold

The field within your arm's authority.

But if you would dismount, what would we see?

I do not think you are a match for me

Or any captain of the Trojan race

On foot." Camilla takes the bait and drops

Before her taunter, one Aunus' son.

He laughs; he turns his steed and rides away

Back toward the line of cavalry from which

He made his bluffing charge. He sees their eyes
Amazed instead of bright with laughter, for
He has not glimpsed Camilla dashing past
His fastest gallop as no other on
The mortal earth could run nor ever ran
Save Hercules, divine Achilles, or
Some other son of gods. But she is none
Of these things: only woman, trained for war.
She's caught him, too, and, eager, stands between
Him and his frightened allies. Axe in hand,
And flush from letting loose her truest speed
She leaps beneath his brave and charging steed
And cuts the leather strap that holds his saddle.
His shaken horse runs free, and he is left
To offer up his neck like firewood
Unto her hungry axe, which loves its work.

BOOK THREE

But Arruns has attended to her work;
He's sore from falling first to her attack.
She should have killed him, but she was so quick
To flit from man to man, and leave none whole.
She should have killed him. But the fates ordained
That he survive and stalk her on the field
And nurse his thoughts of her as Tarquin would
In idle hours nurse Lucretia's name
Within his mind before he looked on her.
(For in his thoughts he'd conquered her already,
And could not fathom that a women could
Prove different in herself than he had willed
That she should be.)
                      And other eyes have seen
Camilla too: the eyes of women who
Now gather at the walls to see which way
The day will turn. Camilla gives them hope,
For here she stands away from city walls,
On foot, flanked by her sister Volscians,
Instructing every man who comes her way
In how an axe is wielded: when a spear
Is thrust at you, you step aside and cleave
Its tip off and then catch the falling blade
And pierce the face of him who lunged at you.

But if he lifts a shield to block your blow,
You use the blade Diana made herself
To shear his shield in two, then crush his skull.
The bodies of the Trojan dead begin
To call the vultures from their waiting trees.
They circle overhead, a distant crown
Upon her work of slaughter.

                        Far away
Aeneas watches her from wooded slopes
And wonders how the walls could ever fall
Into his hands. His opposite within
Those walls, Lavinia, is musing too.
She's heard the rumors of Camilla's work,
And now ascends the battlements and sees
Her dueling Chloreus, whose armor is
A royal golden hue, the finest made
Beside the Tiber's shores. Alas, his sword
Is useless on Camilla's ringing shield.
Amused, she lops his blunted sword in half
And thrusts him backward with her shield; he sees
For just a moment, right before his eyes,
The middle of her shield where hounds are carved
Pursuing some poor man who's angered her
Who blesses every pious hunter with
The prey they seek. Now Chloreus is fox,
Camilla is the hunter, and the prize

Is his audacious armor, which he rues
Himself for ever having made. It weighs
Him down, and she is slashing at his heels
As he is sprinting fast as he can run.
But she is jogging, barely breathing hard,
And felling his companions as she goes:
Poor Buttes, stabbed from behind, and Demophon,
And Tarchon, who had asked the gods to grant
Himself a rampage that would match her own;
But she whips back her bow, stops short,
Gives Chloreus a sporting chance, then plants
An arrow in the raging Tarchon's eye.
She catches up to Chrloreus, beheads him,
Then stoops to strip his armor. See her turn
Her well-trained eyes from where she often scanned
The sky for well-aimed arrows. Now she bends
Her whole attention to the armor that
Reminds her of— —

                    But eager Arruns asked
Apollo for the blessing of his spear.
She didn't see him sneaking up beneath
The shadow of a nearby tree, nor see
His aching strain to heave the spear so hard
That it could reach her. But he did all this,
And, sensing fate's tense turn, Camilla looked
To skyward as the javelin hit home

And knocked her backward, breastbone split, blade deep
And, with each heartbeat, sipping at her blood.
Then Acca was beside her, held her hand
And looked into the dying warrior's eyes.
Camilla struggled, drawing painful breaths.
"How quickly it can end," she said, "the work
You train your life away to someday do.
I pass my place as head of cavalry
To Turnus now. Tell him I held the field,
And made the Trojans and Etruscans quake
To see a woman truly trained in war.
And if Lavinia survives the siege
Of Latium, I send apology
I did not with my own attempt decide
The fate that she must walk. That is her own."
And Acca watched Camilla slip away;
Her eyes were present, then they closed,
Then opened, but were distant, and she said
In nothing more than whispering:
"Her voice." For she, as many men had done
That day, discerned a voice. But for Camilla
It was no hellish word of Hecate,
But rather that beloved voice she heard
When she was sore and weary, and had found
The deepest heart of forests where the god
Of every Amazon who wages war

Most calls her earthly home: Diana's voice—
And it was full of comfort and of praise,
And so Camilla's spirit slipped below.
Then Acca cried, and Volscians gave way
Before the coming onslaught of the Trojans.
But one Etruscan did not join the charge;
The frightened Arruns knew what he had done:
He'd slain by ruses she who'd never fall
Before him in an open contest. Deep
Into the grove below the hills he ran,
And found a little valley where he hid
His shaking self: he told himself he'd won
Tremendous victory, but knew who saw
His acts—not just Aeneas, but the gods
From their Olympian seats. And he despaired.

For great Diana, who has never left
Her servants without justice, watches him
And sighs as only gods can sigh to see
The fate that cannot be revoked played out
In injury to pious mortals. But
She still can carry vengeance out, can hunt
The hunter of her suppliant. She calls
The archer nymph, quick Oris, to her side,
And says to her: "For Arruns there can be
No place to hide. Camilla was my great

Disciple in this age. If women could
Become like her, I'd hope that there could be
A renaissance of worship at my shrines.
But I do doubt it. No, our final act
Within this battle for the soul of Rome
Will be to send to Arruns his desert."
So Oris rushes down the winds that blow
Across the world, from ruined Troy due west
And over Grecian lands to Italy.
The leaves and flowers of the valley flush
To see her coming, branches bend to brush
Her limbs as she is passing them. Now she
Is closing on poor Arruns; he can sense
He's hunted, but he cannot hear her steps.
He calls out for his allies, and soon finds
A few Etruscan soldiers on patrol.
He thanks the gods, and settles down
His fear. The fool, he does not see the bow
Of Oris aimed, nor how the golden limbs
Are drawn so far they touch each other's tips.
He only hears the arrow as it strikes
His soft and waiting neck. It pierces skin,
Then quaking veins, then moaning throat, then spine,
Then, deep within the neck-bone, all the chords
That join the body into one great whole,
A whole that is the image of the gods.

All this the blade of Oris severs in
One swift, disgusting sound, and right and left
The dying Arruns' allies scatter back
To see him so irrevocably slain.
They deem the gods themselves have sent this death
And leave him bleeding in the lonely dust.

Across the plain Ritullian Turnus sees
The Trojan and Etruscan lines charge toward
The line of Volscians who guard the walls
And precious gate of Latium. He's sat
Upon his charger all this time far from
The gate with his Ritullians to watch
The art of combat which Camilla taught.
He trusted that she'd hold the walls with ease,
And so she did, but now, since Arruns' dart
Has broken, for a moment, the resolve
Of all her Volscians—now Turnus curses
His slowness, for he cannot reach between
Aeneas' cavalry and Latium.

Some Volscians retreat from where they've been
Engaged in combat, wheeling like their queen
And tossing javelins like boys toss balls.
They scramble on their steeds, and run across
The vulnerable, open ground to find

The wall of Latium still solid at
Their backs. The Trojans come; their thundering
Reverberates through Latium, and all
The women watching on the walls are caught
Within the shock of seeing she they loved,
Camilla, dying, and the threat of those
Who killed her tearing down their gates.
The Trojans and Etruscans are in range
To hurl their javelins and hit the walls.
But as they raise them, as the Volscians
Brace for the final impact and the end,
Another volley comes from overhead:
The Latin battlements are bristling with
The points of makeshift spears, for there in arms
Are all the women who have only watched
Till now, but now they are a warrior race
Themselves—they've whittle sharp the handles of
The brooms they swept their rooms with, or have found
Their husbands' hunting spears. Some just hurl rocks
With heft enough to crush a helmet in.
The girls cheer to see the women stand,
And as the men are reeling from the darts
From overhead, the girls charge. One man
Is pierced by spear above and spear in front,
Another blocks a rock with dented shield,
But finds a sword-blade slashing at his gut.

Aeneas sees his cavalry give way
Before the Latins, now turned Amazons,
And smiles a little, for his memory
Holds dear the aid of Penthesilea.
But he must take control, or all is lost.
As he descends across the battle plain,
Another mounts the Latin battlements
As if to meet him, as Hippolyta
Met Theseus upon the Martian rock.
It is Lavinia, and in her hand
She holds a shining lance—her father's lance
That won him, years ago, renown among
The warlords of the seven Alban hills.
Both Turnus and Aeneas see her now,
And Turnus' joy at Latium's defense
Becomes his fear. Diana sees her too,
And loves her courage, hoping that she will
Abandon both her suitors and swear oaths
To chastity for all her mortal life.

But as Lavinia drew back her spear
And aimed it at Aeneas, Venus slipped
Between the princess and her choice
And showed Lavinia her fate:
She'd never pledge virginity at shrines
Nor wed the local prince that Juno loved;

Instead she saw her famous heirs would be
The sons of Venus' son, and in that sight
Lavinia could taste the sweetness of
That Love that once entrapped the god of war
And left him spear-less, ravaged, and in chains.

Translations

(2012–2021)

1. Major Fragments of Sappho

[1]

Aphrodite on your immortal, bright throne,
Please, wise minded daughter of Zeus, I beg you,
Do not sear my sorrowing heart with more hurt,
Mistress of this soul.

As you did with former requests, attend me—
Flee your father's fortress and, yielding, yoke your
Golden cart, your chariot, drawn by flocks of
Sparrows with fleet wings.

Diving down the atmosphere, rear your beaked steeds,
Glide across the darkening heart of earth and
Halt your train at last, in my room, illumined,
Goddess, before me.

Face divine and shining with joy, you asked who
Hurt me, what's the matter with Sappho this time,
How my sorrow could be relieved, reversed, or
Why I had called you.

"Who should I persuade with my wiles," you asked me,
"Who should plead before you to sooth your passions,
Whose abuse has bruised your affections, Sappho?

Who is this cruel one?

"Though you chase them, they will be chasing *you* soon.
Though they shun gifts, they will be giving gifts soon,
Though they don't love, Oh! when my fire ignites them
They will be yearning."

Help me even now; in my pain divorce me
Far from cleaving grief and from murmured gossip.
Burst my longing's bonds—as an ally battle,
Blade drawn, beside me.

[16]

Maybe it's an army on horse, or marching,
Maybe it's a navy that we should call most
Beautiful of things on the black earth—no, it's
Someone you love most.

Look, it's very easy to prove this point to
All: for think of Helen the wayward, greatest
Mortal beauty, blessed with a handsome husband,
Noble and honored:

Still she sailed for love to the Trojan homeland.
What of children? what of her dearest parents?
She forgot them—left them behind . . .
                                         I miss you,
Anaktoria.

Honestly, I'd rather I heard your lovely
Steps, or saw your radiant face again than
Watched an Eastern chariot race, or one more
Tiresome phalanx.

[31]

Seems to me that he is a god-like being,
What's-his-name, the mortal across from you there,
How he tunes himself to your speech like sugar,
How he is drinking

Every giggle, brimming his love. And I can
Plainly feel my heart in its ribcage shudder—
Only takes my glimpsing of you, and then my
Voice is accosted,

Cannot move my idiot tongue, and tiny
Flames, it seems, are teeming within my hot skin.
Eyes can only focus on you, and ears are
Deaf with a drumming.

Bring on cold sweat: quivering, queasy, seized all
Over; blanch me down to a sickly green hue.
Death is barely worse than this horrid feeling,
Let me assure you.

[Brothers]

Don't keep saying Charaxos might as well be
Home, his cargo brimming. It's Zeus who steers the
Fate of men, together with gods. So don't be
Shaping your thoughts so.

Rather you should urge me to make entreaties
To our mother Hera, the queen of mercy,
That my striving brother arrive here quickly,
Steering his own ship

Safe and sound to us who await him. Still, all
This is for the spirits divine to govern.
Lovely weather changes to mighty thunder—
Swiftly the storms come.

So I plead to Lords of Olympus, mighty
Daemons, that they aid us; for those they favor
Find reversals, turn to a happy future,
Harvest a great wealth.

Oh, I wish my brother could lift his heavy
Head, and youthful Larikos grow into a
Noble man—for then from these evils he will
Swiftly redeem us.

[58b]

Live life for the Muse, girls, who is voilet-girt and lovely,
Live earnest for fond songs from the sweet voice of the lyre, children.

For I am become old — what was once delicate skin is wrinkled,
And age has blanched hair that was once black — it is white forever.

My spirit is weighed down with my cares; knees refuse their flexing,
Yes, knees that were once nimble as swift fawns in their skips and
        dancings.

But what can I do? Rail and complain? No, for that's what life is:
No, none can escape age and the slow loss of their youth, not one man.

Just think of Tithonus who Dawn loved, the stories tell us:
For though she absconded him far, even to utmost Earth's end

That man who was once beautiful, once young, was found by time and
Grew grey as the fair goddess, his wife, watched — bereft and deathless.

[168b]

    Now that the moon has descended,
    The Pleiades also, the middle
    Night comes with the plodding hours—
    I lie in my bedroom, so lonely.

2. "On the Metered" (*Eis Ta Emmetra*)

by St. Gregory Nazianzus

I see the many penning, in this life of ours,

A language that's unmetered; they just let it flow

And so erase each faded hour with their strained work

According none a blessing—it's all glottal waste.

This kind of writing's only fit for tyrants' pens,

Who fill their pages and their souls with passion's whims

As sand spreads cross the shore, or Egypt swarmed with flies.

Though such an art might please, it poisons human minds.

We should not be so conquered, this I say: discard

All words but those that God inspired and keep them close;

Become, yourself, a harbor to hold back the storm.

For if our Scripture is the greatest of all words

Then you, my Holy Spirit, with your wisdom may

Craft that Great Writ itself into a harbor for

Those who would flee the strong cacophony of fools.

When you are writing down your dim opinions, do

You treat them, my good friend, as everlasting things?

Such estimation reads creation wrong, mistakes

For Being the fragmented cosmos, which careens

Toward chaos. Each man cuts a wayward path, and leads

Another lonely revolution with his words.

But I have traveled, with *my* words, another road,

And whether beautiful or not, I love it now—

I set down my distress into each metered line,

Neither—as those opiners who recline in sloth

Have thought—to rake in fame, the fickle friend, or gain

A glory wholly hollow. (This is curious:

They rush to criticize my writings, but they work

With that same fame alone as their main goal, and judge

The verse of others by a rubric no one shares.)

Nor do I praise my own creations more than God's;

And would He let me do so? I can't take the thought.

    Thus you may justly wonder why I write at all.

With measured labor—first—I discipline my soul,

For writing lines can order my unmetered mind,

And keep my greedy pen in check—instead I spend

My sweat on metric form. Second, I write for youths,

And for whoever takes a deep delight in words.

My verses read like sugar with elixir mixed;

They can win men to virtue's work and discipline,

By sweetening with art the bitterness of law.

Think how a pulled-back bowstring loves to be let loose!

At least my verse can satisfy your preferences

For popular and lyric compositions. I

Have written hymns and plays for those who wish to play,

But not be hindered in their quest for Beauty. Third—

And if this just sounds petty let me know—I write

To win the current battle which we wage with words;

Where each side seeks, through books, linguistic victory.

(I speak of language that partakes in beauty, though

Supremest Beauty is through contemplation reached.)

Among the worldly wise—the Sophists—we produce

Our faithful plays: now let us act the lion's part.

And fourth, when winter wind brings sickness, struggle, death,

My poems comfort me, swan-like old man; they lull

Me with their wings, embolden me like woodwind hymns—

No threnodies, but songs to lead me ever on.

    Besides all this, you now may know, oh Sophists, what's

Within my heart. But if my words defeat you, would

You give up words, the very matter with which word-

Smiths play? I don't write overlong, obnoxious noise,

Nor useless cant; instead, I've made, I think, what's fit.

The very words can be your teachers if you choose—

Some are my own, some ordered by another hand—

You may find there the Beautiful, or shameful vice,

Dogmatics, gnostic gems, sharp thoughts that slice like knives,

Or words so woven that they make the memory strong.

If mine here seem too brief, expand them till complete.

But *your* verse is malformed by your unmetered self,

And when you make your iambs, each is clipped and blunt.

Those robbed of sight can't recognize the sighted, nor

Can those who hobble keep up with Achilles' pace;

Plus, you can't keep it secret, you who love to blame:

See, what you hate in me, you foster in yourself—

With gross unmeteredness—for you write poetry.

A critic tries to capsize Faith, but she finds port,

And he—fantastic captain—sinks his own fine ship.

A question: do you use such craft, oh Sophists, so

That you might hide your lies and double-mindedness?

An ape you seemed, but now you play the lion's part—

And so the easy love of glory traps one more.

Know this: there is much meteredness in Scripture too,

As wise, old Rabbis of the Hebrew race confirm.

If meter seems to fail you when you pluck the strings,

Contrary to how ancients weaved the song and word,

And crafted chariots of delight from beauteous Good—

What's more, they formed their characters through melodies—

See Saul in his old suffering of the spirit be

Set free internally by David's crying lyre.

Accordingly such ordered pleasures can refresh

The young and lead them back to fellowship with God,

But slow—not raptured quickly to the highest place.

For now, let them be taught by mixtures well begot,

But soon the time will come when beauteous Good inheres,

And like an arch's temporary frame the art's

Removed—then Good alone stands watchman in the soul.

What life of slow becoming profits humans more?

Would a skilled cook leave out the sugar when he bakes,

O solemn ones with sour frowns and stiffened lips?

So don't abuse my well-made meters, and don't judge

Your neighbors' meters by the standards of your own.

Far from Phrygían rivers are Mysían peaks,

As far as lowly crows from heights that eagles reach.

3. Hymns of Ambrose of Milan

Eternal King (*Aeternae rerum conditor*)

Eternal king, conductor of

All things, of day becoming night,

Of times and seasons that relieve

The loathsome weight of all our life.

The rooster, herald of the day,

Now sings—he keeps night-watch for us,

And guides the pilgrim through the dark

When night from night he separates—

At this the dimming morning star

Erases darkness from the sky,

At this the bacchic choruses

Must now desert their witching ways;

At this the sailor musters strength,

His ship-decks tame the fretful sea;

And once, at this, the Church's Rock

Diluted his great guilt with tears.

Now let us surge with strength and stand;

The herald-rooster summons us,

Incriminates our slumber and

Refutes our lazy arguments.

The rooster sings and hope returns,

Disease is rallied on to health,

Each thieving blade is sheathed, and faith

Reverts back to the lapsed once more.

Turn, Jesus, toward the ones who lag

And quicken us with vision, that

The ones who fall may be raised up,

And guilt may be washed clean through tears.

Your light lends fullness to each sense,

Discovers where the mind still sleeps,

Our voices' first, best sonnet and

Our vows are all for you, who save.

Now Comes the Third Hour (*Iam surgit hora tertia*)

Now comes the third hour of the day

When Christ ascended his high cross;

No insults fill the mind, instead

Its cogitations turn to prayer.

He who suspends Christ in his heart

Remains inoculate to harm

And he who prays devotedly,

Receives the Holy Spirit. This

Same hour our Lord met death at last,

Took on our fearful, sluggish crimes;

He trampled lordly death, and then

Abolished guilt from time and space.

Such is the beauty of this hour

When Christ commenced an age of grace:

The one, true faith converts and fills

All churches on this orb of earth.

From his triumphant heights he hailed

Them both, his mother and his friend:

"On your new son, my mother, look;

Apostle, see your mother now"—

He shows, in this, that marriage is

A truth mysterious and high;

The virgin who gives birth will not,

In being mother, be defiled.

The faith that Jesus offers is

Celestial, miraculous,

No credited to impious men,

But to those who believe his creed.

And we believe in God the born,

The sacred virgin's offspring, he

Who bore the world's sins, then sat

Down at the Father's favored side.

Creator Deity (*Deus Creator Omnium*)

Creator deity of all,

And planet-ruler, he who vests

And decorates the day in light,

And covers night in gracious sleep—

There quiet, unencumbered limbs

Rejuvenate for work, there you

Relieve us of our mental wear

And salve our anxious sorrowing.

Now grateful that the day is done

We're called, by night, to prayer, to

Ignite our votive thoughts with flame

And sing out hymns to you who save.

For you our concert-hearts all join

For you we strike our harmonies

To you our spotless loves attach

And you our sober minds adore.

When day drops down, profound, toward night

And darkness spreads across the earth,

The faithful do not recognize

The black, but re-illumine it.

Let minds be never lost in sleep,

Let error be instead removed,

And purest faith make temperate

The frigid vapors of deep sleep.

Reset our slipping senses, let

Our hearts now dream of only you;

Let not our envious enemy

Convert our quietude to pain.

We plead with Jesus Christ and with

His Father, and the Spirit of

Them both—one power shared by all;

We pray your favor, Trinity.

Oh Ruler Guiding Israel (*Intende Qui Regis Israel*)

O Ruler guiding Israel

Who sits above the cherubim,

Appear to Ephrem, exercise

Your strength of potentates and come.

Redeemer of the Gentiles, come

Forth from your virgin mother's womb,

Amaze the spirits of the age—

Such birth is fitting for a God.

Not from a father's virile seed,

But from the Spirit's mystic breath

The Word of God has been made flesh

And fructifies within the womb.

The belly of the virgin swells,

The bounds of purity remain,

And virtue's banner boldly flaps;

God turns within his temple-womb.

Proceeding from that holy place,

The palace of his mother-queen,

The double-natured hero comes

Bestriding highways joyously.

He came forth from his Father, and

Returned back to his Father; He

Adventured through inferno's depths,

Ascended back to heaven's throne.

The ageless Father's equal, clothed,

As with a trophy, with our flesh:

He makes our ailing bodies firm

With virtues of perpetual strength.

Now let Your fulgent manger shine,

And light the night, which breathes anew,

Let darkness never enter it,

Illumined with our lasting faith.

4. Epigrams of St. Kassiani

You know what I really hate? — **12 Epigrams**

I hate the murderer who judges angry men.

*

I hate the cheating spouse who chides the prostitute.

*

I hate the moron miming the philosopher.

*

I hate the wealthy man lamenting like he's poor.

*

I hate the healthy man who shuns the leprous one.

*

I hate conformity in every style of life.

*

I hate the law that does not drip with holy oil.

*

I hate when inquiry is gone and talk remains.

*

I hate to hear instruction where no knowledge is.

*

I hate the sound of silence when it's time for speech.

*

I hate the very richest men who hoard their wealth.

*

I hate the friend of hate who is no friend of God.

It's better (trust me) — *9 Epigrams*

It's better to be lonely than to sin with friends.

*

It's better to be feeble than be fit and evil.

*

It's better to be silent than offend with words;
Such silence never harms and never meets reproach;
It suffers no regret, nor finds itself foresworn.

*

It's better to be poor than to get rich through vice.

*

It's better still to treasure lawfulness than chase
The glow of polished pearls or ringing clink of gold.

*

It's better to have not been born at all than be
A slothful-bodied man who lolls and never walks.

*

It's better far to justly harvest few, small grapes,
Than reap a juicy bounty using unjust means.

*

It's better that you lose than cheat to victory.

*

It's better to procure small beauties temperately
Than beauties overflowing got through lawlessness.

Arroyos:

Sijo and Other Poems

(2015)

I.

Arroyo networks are zones of concentrated geomorphic activity and an understanding of sediment budgets and landscape sensitivity therefore requires a quantitative understanding of their governing mechanisms. A great deal has been written on arroyo networks, particularly those in the u.s. west. . . . Despite these advances, we still lack a quantitative, process-based theory of arroyo formation and development.

   —Gregory E. Tucker, 'Modeling the Dynamics of Gully and Arroyo Formation', 2004

Books

There is a feeling   just before you read

the next book   that will fill a blank

in your thoughts, or form   the formless,

wherever it is   in you: a sense that

your ignorance knows   it is mortal. It

pins your mind   to the moment, says,

"I am the patient   before the doctor's

news. I am the will   before it is forced

to choose. You will not   ever be

as you are again."   Take your time. It's fine.

Books are patient with   those about to lose.

Arroyos

We have just begun   to understand them:

why sometimes banks split   and swollen rivers

flash out into new   and fractal tracks; why grazing-land

in one morning can   become a fractured grid of floods.

This quick crack is called   *incision*, a fact

known though not quite grasped   by monks, who,

looking back upon   the godless lands they've travelled, gasp

to see a maze of   souls caved in with faith.

Autumn Sijo

1.

Homes and autumns force arroyos   in the clay bank of the mind.
What can be done for me, gouged as I am?   These things I conceive
are brittle contraptions   containing, I hope, a little rapture.

2.

Seven silhouetted pines,   six thousand bricks stacked to form
St Peter's steeple—   so slow at dusk do such sights heal the soul.
Have mercy on the cliff face   through the shine of each slim moon.

3.

A cry skims the brisk Swiss wind.   The gray haired cyclist and his bike are splayed beside the dented Fiat.   His face—half skidded blank— is turned from me. This pain is not *problem*.   It is *mystery*.

4.

Above the walking bridge to Leuchars station   wide raindrops like maple leaves spin   and wobble in the dim October breeze. My gut's pain and my cheek's chill are eased   by eighteen golden streetlamps.

5.

Autumn gathers into shadows   between branches of the pine moulded in iron on the fireplace grill.   What strength have casters mixed with paint that green might gain   a bright proximity to flame?

Meditation in an English Garden

Here one expects certain order: green lattices which
lead straight rows of chive   down pebbled paths which
march from mum to thyme.   But one finds uncut
hedge-tops jagging into autumn   air. Dim clouds cast chill
in unmetered gusts and gravel   boasts no rounded edge.

Tomato globes on   knuckled vines.
Dangled snails. The marsh-ward flop of   berry clot:
an order natural,   too, to human thought.

Superstitions

Would it be   impious to pray:

'Lord, have mercy on   my poem'?

She's so slight,   so hemmed in by white,

that I fear for her   out there near

the gutter puddles,   shuffled from post box

to stack, just to be   undressed by

the hurried hands of   editors, then asked

to quickly perform,   or to last.

So protect her, please.   Bring her to

one who will sit with her, listen,   fold her like

a prayer   between leaves.

Winter Sijo

1.

Why do we stay alive?   To tend to time, to shepherd the kicking year, and play vaquero when it bucks.   Bring me that map with fifty-two countries.   This evening we sail to the utmost East.

2.

On the sidewalk a chunk of moss   sits as if fresh-ripped from rock.
A patch of new-rolled asphalt steams   like a Clydesdale's flank.
In the morning butcher's truck hang three sides of beef   as tall as men.

3.

Now I see who leaves   these three-toed prints in morning snow—
It's you, fat crow.   Did you know that I too walk light, afraid
I may break some delicate white   given to earth by the night?

4.

If my skin were born of North Wind   I wouldn't weary, as I do,
Of week on week of rain.   You, my complaining soul, are like
A ruffled monarch, who seeks a southland   dry as flaming sage.

5.

How to write about this place: swing from a pub-sign, clamber
Up a stone façade, cup   a chimney between chin and throat and wait.
Your pores will open.   Your torso will steam like an Edinburgh roof.

Carriage: An Elegy

And as we left Los Angeles   an oak leaf came, on

Griffith Lane and snagged   our truck's antenna in its thorns.

If it stays, I thought,   *then so will the child.*

Sun, burst; and models,   twirl. Moon, clip light; stars,

whirl your pinholes in   night's leather glove which cups these hills.

To you asteroids too,   you who fell from universal

to sidereal time—   I've come to say I'm gone.

Vendor, grill for me   one last meal.

Wrap it in bacon,   onion, crème.

Consumer,   observer,

subsumer,   conserver,

you city of a hundred names—   *Because the leaf did not remain—*

Goodbye. Where are you,   Junipero Serra? I've come

To make confession.   Slide a white-oak screen

between us   and I will tell you:

Because the leaf did   not remain,

because it sloughed off   in the wind

of August, I knew   the child was lost.

El Pueblo   De Nuestra Señora

La Reina   De Los Angeles,

I will carry, carry, carry   the scent of you east.

I pluck *conserver*   from your hundred names—

this is how we came   to Edinburgh: humbled, craving rain.

II.

Though snow-flakes may cover him   the crow's black coat does not
    blanch white.

The night cannot darken the light of the moon.   And though these
    worries

pile and pile, please tell me: why I should lose my loyalty to my lord?

                  —Bak Pengnyeon, 15th-century Korea

Two Nativities

    —From the Greek of St Romanos the Melodist

1. *The Nativity of the Theotokos*

Joachim and Anna   the disgraced, the childless ones
    have freed Adam and Eve   from the corruption that death wrought,
    have released them, making death useless,   by bringing forth a holy one, you;
your parents join all those   who crowd around you,
    soldiers subject to stumbling,   who shout out this salvation song:
"The barren one bears   the bearer of God,   she who nurses us back to life."

2. *The Nativity of Christ*

Today the virgin gives birth   to him who is beyond being,
    and in the cave the earth   meets the unreachable heavens;
angels above are creating   glory in language,
    magi below make their journey,   chasing down starlight;
for through her he   has now been born.
    Such a small child   is God—who outstrips the ages.

Belated Spring

    1.

The trees are weary   of appearing dead.
Lean as Lent, long crows   perch hatchlingless on shadowed boughs.
But onto the plowed field now   the pheasant steps, decked
as if a Qahar artist   had upset his pallet
on her neck and all   the heraldry of changing years

had spread until her body was   a calendar on
which, from bone-gloss beak   to stippled feather, one might read
the story of the furrowed earth   from birth to bursting.

    2.

From birth to burst our history   is rimmed with light, and
that clysmic flash at   its end will be, some say, hellfire,
others, nova-glow.   But I am warming
to the thought that there is, beyond   all lights, a sun that
gives them life, and we   who feel so concrete, little else,
are favorite concentrations of   an energy so

different from   the abstract hate of flame that some

have dared to   call it by God's name.

Abra, Age 8, Visits St. George's Cathedral

I stole it,   a piece of the Prophet Isa

from the bearded priest   at Maura's church. He

said the Prophet is   the wine-soaked bread. I

stood in line behind   Maura, repeated

her words to the priest: *Handmaiden of God*.

He spooned Isa into my mouth.   My two lips hid him.

When I arrived home   he was mush, but I

dried him out all night.   Three round crumbs were left.

If only mother   had not dusted. I was going

to keep him near me,   to taste him sometimes—when I cry,

or my mouth is moist with hunger.   I even thought that

Imam Hassad would like a piece.   At Masjid I could

drop it in his palm.   He is holy. He   would know who it is.

Spring Sijo

1.

Out from the charcoal angles of a close   cherry branches peek;

The careful buds look both ways down North Bank Street   then plume pink.

The elder Sunni wraps an emerald   hijab round her neck.

2.

Has the light-pole in St Patrick Square   always looked like a pike?

New chimneys seem gun-barrels bundled by nines.   What stealthy saints

have lately worked this peace?   Who beats our swords to streetlamps while we sleep?

3.

Spring poppies, please shock me   that I may remember not your red
but your return.   Teach me hope, for I die like you, like you
I am revived.   He is the god of all redounding lives.

4.

A newly pregnant womb   like the bread in a young priest's cup
contains a life to which we're not attuned.   But do you hear?
The bird-song is so bright tonight   it must be coming from the moon.

5.

Some evenings the second hand creeps toward twelve,   other nights it sprints
while Chong-Ch'ol's sijo sit untranslated on shelves,   while ripe
> and swelling bellies wait the crowning of the child, while undeclared anduncompleted wars still litter Western desks, while El Camino Real lies unadorned by shrines, while the internationale still stirs the soul that has renounced it, while the poor, the proud, the pure, the pained, the college and the mall all share one city-space, while as of old we still record each season in three lines—

I chase, I tell you, a still spring morning   full of one clear thought.

The California Condors

    —For Nonna Verna Harrison

The way of dodos was their way,   improbable birds

fated to fall from   Darwin's leaf-stripped tree.

But man, it turned out,   had wings within him:

with care he captured   each great vulture, made

a sanctuary   for their slow healing.

He stitched a likeness   of a condor's form

to feed the mother-   deprived nestling, to remind it

what sort of being   it could still become.

Such rescue is what   church can be:

in rooms lined   with likenesses we

succor a deep and   endangered wingspan,

discover and clean   forgotten feathers

tangled in the dark   flesh of every chest.

Marriage

The difficulty   of the dance
respects the dancers.   There, for once,
the form is so well   suited to the flesh
that every quality of self   may find place
in the pattern, with   none left, or borrowed

by some other art.   I gather up the
stumbles of my heart   and grind them on the
stone of your   steps' answers.
Thus, allied with time,   the difficulty
of the dance   perfects the dancers.

Summer Sijo

1.

Tonight the crescent moon ascends   the top branch of the sycamore.

From there it leaps to St Peter's steeple and   clinging on

with pointed claws   howls back at watching wolves a summer song.

2. *At the Grave of St Bede*

The man beneath this slab has been   for me a flashbulb in

time's dim eclipse. I scrape   the shadows from your shrine, blessed Bede,

I sharpen these weak eye-beams on   your tomb's rough, Roman glyphs.

3.

August fills the evening air;   I whisper into mist and heat,

I've still not found your song.   One weary gull above this wing-clogged street

finds a wind-drift east   and pulls all summer with him toward the sea.

4.

So make of me a timber-wolf   to sing against the summer's wane, to write

a ballad, bold as Shield-Danes,   for August. Tell me, are

the pumpkins ripe?   I'll pull their pulp-strings taut, pluck them like a lyre.

5.

September shoulders in   bringing with him cloud-shine, shiver.

The last waves of summer   raise their humming weight against the dark.

Autumn is an infant: *make new room,* it says, *for me in your heart.*

The Martyr, the Grizzly, the Gold:

Poems

(2012)

I. Golden Sonnets

"[Q:] How many pairs of rabbits can be produced from a single pair if every month each pair begets a new pair which from the second month on becomes productive?
[A:] 0, 1, 1, 2, 3, 5, 8, 13, 21..."
— Leonardo "Fibonacci" of Pisa, from Liber Abaci, 1202.

"California is a place . . . in which the mind is troubled by some buried but ineradicable suspicion that things had better work here, because here, beneath that immense bleached sky, is where we run out of continent."
— Joan Didion, "Notes from a Native Daughter"

Of My State

If I were a wanderer
I'd tote a book-worn, canvas pack,
A leather coat, a prayer rope,
And I would make my pilgrim path
Among your poppies in the spring,
The gold that splashes on your hills
And keeps your freeways company.
California, you're a condor,

And I cannot write
Why I love you yet,
Why you call these feet
To leave this small room,
Chase you like a lark.

The Lark

Two unasked ornaments—we receive them
Christmas morning from our father:
A cardinal, crimson for my
Brother, and for me a lark:
Wire feet to perch on branches,
Golden faced, brown-striped, flanked in pink.
I've looked for such larks but never
Seen any so colored, so still.

And now you may know
That I am a lark,
But if real or fake
I can't say—look at
My face—is it gold?

The Canyon, Age 8

Though we've never heard the word before,
Dad calls this fort we've built "The Delf."
It's just three two-by-fours in branches,
Covered in thick plywood. And I learned
A second word today from Dad
When a beam fell, hit his head, and
"Shit!" slipped from his mouth. He points out
White pellets on the ground below.

He says owls vomit
Out their food each night—
It comes out white.
I perch, a little owl,
Tasting my new words.

Sillion

It was the mattock's tail that scared me,
Its rust-red paint scoured by clods 'till
Silver and smooth. When swung point first
It dislodged rock, ripped trenches for
Planting or play. But I swung shy,
Remembered Cree's story: christened
Charles, but baptized in his own sprays
Of rust, uprooting stumps at 12—

His gritting father
Had to brace a foot
Against his still chest
To pry the eager
Mattock from his eye.

Hardware

I fluttered fingers down the links
Of rippled chain on plywood wheels
Scooped palms full of drywall nails
As Dad bought dusty, white mulch bags
And spools of orange, weed-eater line.
Past hardware and checkout counter
He called me—but as I followed
To our truck cab's heavy heat,

My breath was still
In the bin of screws,
Their metal scent
Becoming summer
In my aging chest.

Youth Outing

The wind laps lake Nacimiento;
My kayak scoops small waves. On shore
Sarah finally fills that suit,
yellow, with lace-whorled cups
And every eye keeping time with
Her breathing. I drift, wait for my
Arms to quit their ache, probe the oaks
For signs of life, smell sunrays age.

Light—She sinks in slow,
Wakes Autumn's mud from
August drought, drains youth
From our forms until
We are old as She.

Ricardo Montalban, In Memoriam

    –for BGII

The Anaheim rooftops are tongues

Curled up to taste the tamarind

Sucker of late summer sunset,

And I drive home, over the concrete

Grave-slabs of the 5 freeway, over

The skin-brown soil which catches breath

At off-ramp or median—you

Breathed this hard air too Ricardo, past

Your rich Latin tongue,

Early dark star of

That once white screen. Sleep.

For now, even this

Sun grows bronze with glee.

Degrees

August ends and Angeles forest
Is filled with flame, smoke blooms cumulus
Above the flu-sick city
And daylight hasn't dropped below
100 for a thirsty week.
Your fever broke at midnight as
Our fan hummed lukewarm in the hall;
I watched the San Gabriels glow

And hoped that they—with
Air, with day—could slow
Their bright dance and meet
By low degrees your
Body's sleeping heat.

Metaphors

November's moon is a searchlight
Scanning ground from helicopter
Height; it catches streets red handed,
Trees loitering after-hours
In parks, and me, in moccasins
And white undershirt heaving
Recyclables into the common
Dumpster—all of us thieves. Or, even

The police searchlight
Is a November
Moon, waxing over
This city with no
Warrant more than joy.

A Baptism at Epiphany

Henrik, before you were thrice dunked,
Before you yelled with gums flushed red,
You arched your naked back in my hands,
And gaped against my chest for breast
Milk. Your infant eyes could not see
The altar near, nor the candle
Which flicked before an icon of
A child Christ. When you wanted

Milk, the priest gave you
Water. But Christ wept
With you, his tongue a
Wick, flaming with a
Hot and holy cry.

St. Thomas's Chemistry Lesson

The ancients' elements were earth,
Air, fire, water. Bohr split those
To bits, and any breath or dust
We dip our modern fingers in
Teems with multitudes—Hydrogen
Boron, Oxygen, Tin—flakes, some say,
To build the snow-bank of the world with.
But I doubt these rumors, and wait for

The elements of Spring:
A certain body
And a certain blood,
Which, if alive, are
My Lord and my God.

Spring Disjunctive

Disneyland finches chirp rapid,
A man leans camera-phone first
Over orange birds of paradise,
And, while other gold dressed Belles
Pout or ask for toys with smiles,
One little, Down's swelled princess plods
Pink and expressionless. Premises:
Either she knows she is clad in

Magic or she is
Oblivious. She
Is oblivious.
Conclusion:
You are that girl.

II. The Martyr

The Shaman

"The following is a translation of the readable passages from the instructive writings of Ach-Goyan, late shaman of Kodiak Island, the text of which I discovered, along with a pectoral crucifix, in his hut on my first missionary visit to the Aleut village at Akhiok, Advent 1824. I believe the passages, while simple and often redundant, will be of interest to those researching the shamanic arts."

– Brother Alexei of St. Herman's Monastery, Forefeast of Pentecost, 1866

1. Beasts

Each young shaman must remember
Beasts are often humans hidden
Under pelt and paw — a warrior
Who has shown great fear in battle,
Or who stole his brother's weapon —
These men's souls may be imprisoned
By the Spirits in a beast.

Each young shaman must remember
Beasts like seals and dolphins are your
Wayward brothers in disguise —
When you hunt them, sing a love song,
When you spear them, whisper soft:

Now my friend, my hidden soul-friend,
Bleed your way out of that prison.

2. Spirits

When they die, all wise men's spirits
Leave their bodies, but remain to
Hover in the air and water,
Waiting to protect their nephews:
Those of us who seek to match them,
Those of us who wear amulets
Crafted from a rush or pebble.

Each young shaman must remember
How to braid the rush and pebble,
How to swab the spit from dying
Wise men for the young to swallow.
If you craft these rites the spirits
In the wind will whisper soft:
Now, my friend, my bodied soul-friend,
Hunt the lovely quarry, wisdom.

3. Strangers

Each young shaman must remember
The two reasons why the stranger

Is revered among our people.
First, our uncles once were strangers
Paddling lost canoes on oceans,
Led by Sedna, the sea goddess,
To this island to learn wisdom.

Second, shamans long ago
Prophesied the moon-skinned stranger,
Prophesied his coming to us,
Prophesied his ways becoming
Our ways also. Shaman, listen
To the story of my folly,
Folly and the moon-skinned stranger:

4. Story

Paddling his canoe from northward
Came a stranger to our island,
Skin of moon and beard of otter.
Just before his boat scraped shore,
I released my waiting bowstring.
Other warriors, hid in bushes,
Followed, filled his chest with arrows.

Shaman, if you know this, tell me
Why his wounded arm kept pointing

Skyward, then—as if horizon,
And not he, was dying—swept his
Hand across as if to soothe it?
I have seen the dyings' actions,
Seen them gurgle out their spirits,

Seen them flail as if for pity,
But this stranger stepped out of his
Boat, and though he dyed the pebbles
Red, approached us as an uncle
Would an injured, favorite nephew,
Making all the time those gestures.
Shaman, do not do as I did,

Do not give the warlike order
To dismember that wise stranger,
Do not raise the war-club, do not
Crush his totem-making arm
If you see the wisdom in his
Eyes. Above all, do not take the
Amulet from round his broken neck.

Laughing that I took it from him,
Wearing it upon my chest, I
Called upon surrounding spirits
As I dripped the spit on dusk fires—

But I conjured only silence,
And, as if there were no spirits,
I could make no spark of magic.

The Bankrupt's Prayer

Numbers, once so constant, blur and slip
through the zero they were born from—
they were only pixels, only
forms in ink—the spaces between
the spinning stars remain. Shadows,
merge round me with dim pinions
while I ring this belfry of shells;
wing me from this hollow wheel

to a place still blank
and fortuneless.
My gods! Let this
slim bullet light my
empty skull with suns.

Peter the Aleut

      1.

I'll let you know this one up front:
Peter dies; he's disemboweled. You
needn't keep reading. It wasn't called
Alaska then, but that's where he
was born. In some icons you'll see
little Peter in mission school,
and tall Herman, in red and gold
teaching from an open text while

the Kodiak mountains jut above
a frozen sea. As far as northern
legend tells us, Peter led a band
of trappers South to San Francisco.
But, while exploring oak and bay,
they were captured by Franciscans
who bound them, pressed them to recant
the teachings of the Russian monks.

"I am a Christian" Peter said.
"I will not betray my faith."
They crushed his ankles, one by one,
cut off his fingers. He renounced

nothing. They slit him open,
silent as a doe among the oaks.
Some say the coyotes mourned him.
Some say the sun-brimmed hills turned red.

2.

Dad hung his lung shot
sow from the third rung
of the steel windmill
down the canyon from
our rust-stuccoed ranch.

He said the pig breathed
wide bubbles of blood
as she went down. Now
her mouth just trickled
into sticky grass.

He passed knife through hide,
sliced skin in strips from
fat, then fat from muscle,
then all that from bone,
left a ribcage ripe

with dying organs,
still draining out the
fly-thick, clotted mouth.
The scent of all this
was the richest I've known.

3.

Once Monterey got news of the mess,
and deemed the Russian threat not worth
the killing of such heretics,
the monks freed Peter's trapping band,
who brought the news of Peter's words
and death to Herman, hermit-saint,
confessor of all Kodiak,
who used a plank as a blanket.

When he heard the tale I've told
he burned a fir-resin incense,
knelt, and prayed before an altar;
there, on a thin, pine plank, painted
with pigment and egg, a God
slowly died with a spear-slit side.
Then Herman named Peter a saint
with "Holy Peter, pray for us!"

No Spanish sources mention any
of this. Only the Russians,
who, disappointed with poor trade
in California, their far east,
left that pagan coast to Spain—they
remember Peter on the cusp

of Fall, when leaves flush at hunting
season. And I only write this to say:
that was the richest scent I've ever known.

III. Exalt!

These things, these things were here, and but the beholder
Wanting.
    — G.M. Hopkins

To Moonrise

Up! Swollen shadow-
Scape, orange flushed face, black
Browed, yellow chinned, past
Shimmer-dim ribbon
Haze—rise, brighten, blanche

And blue you
Silver mouth
Exalting.

To the Mammoth

Let limber light
Unslumber your tar
Slung limbs, rehinge each
Socket to ball joint,
Lumber up all tusk

And lobe—hulk
Broad above
Black earth's blood.

To Raindrops

Belly-fetch the dusk
Won from fog-sopped eaves—
Spool her silver cold
Within your swinging
Bulb—Swerve, wobble, plash

And plume these
Mercury
Blooming streets.

To Headlights

Such life-like brisk eyes
Winter-bright but blurred,
Pixeled with slurring
Tides of mist—you dip,
Slide, and rise just as

Two herons
Bear their curved
White bulks high.

To the Donut Shop

Sell me 50 cent
Cigarettes, lotto
Boasting host—drip brew
The early dawn dark,
Glaze day in maple,

Noon in pink,
Evening in
Thick slow sleep.

To Game Night

Shine our brittle steins
With lager, charge our
Shouting mouths with light,
Loose a red balloon
To rise past splashing

Fireworks up
To summer's
Storm-dark heart.

To Japan

Bob in throbbing waves
That frame famed Fuji
You June-rain renga
Chain—lay your ink gaze
On my horizon,

These stanzas
Are stones for
Your islands.

To Sunset

Smolder, you golden

Garland, flora flare,

Immortal mortar

Lobbed from god-helmed guns.

Taurus' holy nose

Sweating wet

Neon—you

Root earth's air.

To the Grizzly

Hulk of muscle, trunk, and ribcage,
Still your shifting skin can skim on
Ligaments over your bulk. Mine
Can too, but bare, hairless, a cinch
To shear with claw or jaw.
                        As a boy
I heard of the hunter you mauled,
Who kept his scalp from sliding down
His face with a tight, red ball cap.
From fear of this we shot or caught you,

Tied you to a stake,
And bet that bull or dog
Could break your carp-starved,
Fighting, fighting frame.

On the Road

    —after Goethe

You who ask this open sky
To ease your grief, allay your pain,
To remove your misery
And fill you up with light again—
Ah, I am beat just like you.

What carved out this ache in us?
Tonight, old rest,
Come—oh, come—and heal this chest.

To the Reader, from the Hermit
    — after St Gregory the Theologian

With exalting I came from suppressing my flame,
A moth, a husband holding holiness as wife,
For I have found Sophia's foremost fountain:
Abstinence—wisdom's deepest spring and sweetest drink
By which I left my self and shuddered at my state.
How can you help me, a hermit? Increase your thirst;
Pray—through even this you become my companion,
For you can extinguish great flames in your self, and
If you attain this you also will understand God.

The Gold

California's golden like this:
A bulb-hot sun, and when rain comes
It's greedy, mine-rush rain from fits
Of silver-loded clouds grieving
Evening mist, punched with fists of light.
It's a rough and crumble flash-tan
Land, a star blanched asphalt, moss-grown
Oak bark, summer hill-gilt land. I wish

I had some skin-shine,
That sun would gold my
Two eyes, my cold mind
Trying to heave and hold
The horizon line.

Of My State, 2

I've tried to know it, to sit at
Lake Cachuma's shore, oaks weaving
Their thick-barked boughs with air behind
My back, before me some poems,
Past them the lake's slender waves
Lapping like lyric stanzas, and
Beyond far hills the mission chain
Giving way to San Francisco

Where pines still grow from
Peter's blood soaked soil,
Where Bishop John once
Lifted hands in blessing
Like a red, red bridge.

Four Counties

(2011)

1. Ventura

In our elder teenage days, we low-church children seldom prayed, but pastors
put podiums before us, where we spoke profane before the youth, cursed about
their need for righteousness and fervent, God-filled lives. And there were nights

we stumbled in contemplation of the ancient language of lamplight
in dusk puddles when our minds too were muddled with ale and theology.
We acted the scholar on Saturday late mornings, poring over Saint Paul,

fixed on caffeine and the highest law of right doctrine—though food and sleep
seduced us in the early afternoon. We wanted to be free, but were evening beasts
unshaven, a gospel to coastal baristas and beach bartenders. And there were

nights strong-headed girls lassoed our glances, sipped our senses
and our words with western graces, saying, "Come and sit with me; eat
my opinions; I'll drink yours until we are full of moonlight

and the movement of our wills against each other's—again, again, again
until my mind conceives a new, more beautiful will." We went with them,
those sirens, intoxicate, surf-bound, bent by books. Did we die in drains at
       midnight

and rise undead at dawn—animals, disciples, vow-broken Jesuits,
brought to our knees by strange beauties—sighing, longing, begging beneath
the budding sun, frantic to that face: "Will we ever be human again?"

2. Los Angeles

And we shot half-meant glances toward the crook-necked Cathedral,
flared our eyes with freeway paint and Guadalupe's light, but drove on past
to Sunset where the music always blooms. And there, as if an earthquake

shook our shoulders, we turned to see men wide-eyed, holy, proffering
crosses on sidewalks crowded with gray flannel, the pink chiffon of business,
and belly drunk vagrants who may be angels, we remembered, and still

the cassocks swayed before us with the offer of the image bearer's office
and we took it; we peeled the muraled Jesus off our Christian college walls
to plaster our bodies with color— pink of flesh to match our flesh, red of word

to match our blood, and the deep, heaving blue of space, blue of shroud, blue
of depths from which Christ steps to transfigure or to resurrect. And in our
second decades' dawn we dared to call on God, and our ears were opened

to a thousand races sunk and braying from La Brea's pits. And we were called
to beggar our bodies, silence our minds, trust that in such deserts we could learn
      at last
to live, to pray, to "become in body as a corpse, and in spirit as the seraphim,"

and under the arch where Guadalupe pleads, the holy father said: "You are not
too far from God." But we felt so far from ourselves, far from that farm
of low loves where we prodigals once purged away our souls beside the swine.

But we swore to be no more a mad generation—but a generation waiting

for the words to learn to pray, the time to be redeemed, the smog to be rolled
> back,
and a patch of glory to light the eyes of every sinking beast.

3. Riverside

By the waters of Elsinore we sat down and wept—for the profane, the proud,
the university, the mist between the world and us, stains and scratches
on the city sky. We sit and weep and if any man hears our voice,

let him leave us to our California ramblings, to our teeth grinding at midnight
while the moonlight makes a thousand children smile. Come,
it is time to lift our eyes past the clouds that hold the slopes

of mountains in duress, past the beams which fall through furrowed clouds down
upon the water, past the mist waltzing with light on the crowded dance-floor of
      air, time
to move our mouths and say: *For the peace of the world and for the salvation*

of our souls, let us pray: Holy John, spook of Shanghai, ghoul of godless'
nightmares, etched in egg on plaster walls, scouring San Francisco with your
      bliss
and hyssop, flinging tracts and anathemas into summer air: pray—

Pray for us local boys who fling bottles into the blinding drink, arcing rainbows
of spit and lager. Pray for us catechumen youth, giggling through the grammar
liturgy of "aurum: gold, argentum: silver," mistranslating sanctus as "scared."

Pray for the profane, the proud, the university, and all these things
which make their home in me. Pray for the parasailors gambling with
the California wind, high above Elsinore, even with mountain-tops—they have
      risen

Of their own accord, over mankind's strange addictions in the summertime of loves,
but oh, how sailors yearn to raise their brothers, to have the holy flame and strength
to fling man skyward and populate the heavens with a splay of soaring stars.

4. San Luis Obispo

Vineyards sipped the hillsides of our childhood, tailpipes toked air, and both
        paled
to that gray I chased in a dozen girls' eyes and found, at last, in yours.
For lately we stood, hands clasped by the cliffs' deft edge and pledged

our bodies to an ancient fast, and hearts to an older God. And I asked you
for your hand within that secret grove where gray leaves gather on the ground
and tiny spiders roam. You did not see it, but a red fox ran

the trail before us, his silver tipped tail flitting past oak roots, and you
wound the white gold round. Remember, then, that rich eighth day
when we wed with fall full fledged about us, when the redwood rafters

which witnessed seven generation's prayers—the wife who prayed to stop
Spain's war, the padre who sought a quiet mind, the miner who asked for a glint
in the river, the union who pledged dry hands and ink-wet votes together—

those eyes, those axe split pine knots watched our sacrament too,
and resounded in their inner rings when the bishop called all creatures of our God
and King to sing in wonder at our offering.
                                  When we forget all that we vowed

those long beams know, that gray grove knows, the river's shore,
the asphalt plaza, and this gold horizon know—that these ends of earth
have seen men that shed their molting selves and prayed.

Acknowledgements

New Poems:

"Status Check" was originally published in *Curator Magazine* in August 2019.

"Canceled" was originally published in *Solum Journal*, Vol, 1: Fall 2020.

"The Old Craftsman" was originally published in *Solum Journal*, Vol, 1: Fall 2020.

The poems in "Micro-sapphics" originally appeared as part of my Twitter Chapbook Project in April 2019. They were subsequently collected into the digital chapbook *#April*.

"Too late or not too late" was originally published in *Solum Journal*, Vol, 1: Fall 2020.

Section 3 of "Autumn Elegiacs" was originally published under the title "Extinction Elegiacs" in *Dreams and Nightmares* 117, January 2021.

"Which Way I Fly" was originally published in *Solum Journal*, Vol, 1: Fall 2020.

"The Servant of the Architect" was originally published in *The Pointed Circle* XXXIV, 2018.

"A Crown for Abba Moses" was originally published in *This Present Former Glory: An Anthology of Honest Spiritual Literature* (A Game for Good Christians, 2020).

Book One of "The Camillad" was originally published in *Illuminations of the Fantastic* Issue 8, February 2021.

Translations

"On the Metered" was originally published in *Saint Katherine Review* 4.2, 2014.

"Oh Ruler Guiding Israel" was originally published on The Saint Constantine School blog, December 2017.

Arroyos: Sijo and Other Poems

All poems in this section were published in a chapbook in 2015 by Mariscat Press. Selected poems originally appeared in various periodicals, listed below:

"Books" and "The California Condors" were originally published in *Transpositions*. "Books" was also featured in *The Scotsman* newspaper.

"Arroyos" was originally published in *Pilgrimage*.

"Superstitions" was originally published in *Windhover*.

"Spring Sijo 2" was originally published in *Dreams and Nightmares*.

"Abra, age 8" was originally published in *The Christendom Review*.

"Summer Sijo 5" was originally published in *Curator*.

The Martyr, the Grizzly, the Gold

All poems in this section were published in a chapbook in 2012 by Damascene Press. Selected poems originally appeared in various periodicals, listed below:

"The Lark" was originally published in *Zocalo Public Square*.

"The Canyon, Age 8" and "The Bankrupt's Prayer" were originally published in *The Other Journal*.

"A Baptism at Epiphany" and "St Thomas's Chemistry Lesson" were originally published in *Saint Katherine Review*.

"Peter the Aleut" was originally published in *Christianity and Literature*.

The first eight poems in part III, "Exalt," appeared as a digital chapbook in 2017.

Four Counties

All four poems were originally published in *Relief Journal* 5.2, 2011.

Notes

"St Basil Chapel" contains references to the Chapel of St. Basil on the campus of University of St. Thomas, Houston, designed by Philip Johnson in 1997. The crucifix installation mentioned in the poem was a collaboration between Johnson and Dominique de Menil.

Micro-Sapphics: The form of these poems is an adaptation of the Sapphic stanza. The first two lines consist of a dactyl and a trochee, and the third line consists of two trochees. Spondaic substitutions have been made when fitting.

"The Servant of the Architect" is a fictionalized account of the murders that took place at Frank Lloyd Wright's Taliesin House in 1914. It is written from the perspective of the murderer, Julian Carlton.

"A Crown for Abba Moses" retells seven events from the hagiography of St. Moses of Ethiopia. A more complete account of his life can be found in the *Sayings of the Desert Fathers*.

"The Camillad" is an amplified retelling of the rampage of Camilla from Book 11 of Virgil's *Aeneid*.

Major Fragments of Sappho include seven of the most complete fragments of poems by Sappho from the 6th century BC. Two of these fragments, "[Brothers]" and "[58B]," were only recently discovered, in 2014 and 2004 respectively. In my translations I have attempted to retain in English meter the basic form of Sappho's Greek lyric meters.

"On the Metered" is a poem by St. Gregory Nazianzus, likely written in the 380s AD in Cappadocia. The central section of the poem, where Gregory presents his four reasons for writing poetry, is one of the most important passages of early Christian literary theory. I have attempted to retain in English meter the iambic trimeter (three sets of double iambs) of Gregory's Greek.

The Hymns of St. Ambrose include all four of the indisputably authentic hymns of St. Ambrose of Milan from the 380s AD. These hymns are among the most influential in Christian history, consisting as they do of relatively clear and simple meditations on Christian life and theology in the memorable iambic tetrameter quatrain form. This approach to hymnography was invented by Ambrose and has been imitated by Western hymn writers from late antiquity to the present day. I have attempted to retain in English meter the iambic tetrameter of Ambrose's Latin.

Epigrams of St Kassiani include poems from two sequences of gnomic verse written by the poet-abbess Kassiani in 9th century Constantinople. Kassiani wrote many epigrams beginning with the same phrase, in this case "I hate" and "It's better." I have attempted to retain in my English translations the basic rhythm and length of Kassiani's lines.

Arroys: Sijo and other Poems contains many poems written in the Korean *sijo* form. The sijo arose in Korean literature in the 14th century and consists of three lines of 14–16 syllables each. Though sijo are not as well known in English as the similar Japanese haiku form, Korean literature is filled with literary masterpieces in the sijo form. Perhaps the greatest of the sijo poets was the 16th century poet Chong Ch'ol, whose work deserves more attention in the Anglo-phone world.

"Two Nativities" include translations of the first stanzas, or *troparion*, of the hymns (*kontakia*) for the Nativity of the Mother of God (*Theotokos*) and Christ. These hymns were written by St. Romanos the Melodist in 6th century Constantinople, and are still sung in the Orthodox Church on September 8th (Nativity of the Theotokos) and December 25th (Nativity of Christ).

The Martyr, the Grizzly, the Gold contains references to several Orthodox saints of North America, including St Juvenaly the Protomartyr, whose martyrdom is retold in a slightly fictionalized way in "The Shaman," and St John of San Francisco, who is mentioned in "Of My State, 2" and in the "Riverside" section of *Four Counties*. Most importantly, major events from the hagiographies of saints Peter the Aleut and Herman of Alaska are retold in "Peter the Aleut."

Golden Sonnets are a form I invented in 2008 as part of a project to imagine new ways to apply the Fibonacci sequence to poetic form to create golden ratios between lines and stanzas. The resulting form is an adapted sonnet, consisting of eight lines of eight syllables each followed by five lines of five syllables each.

"To Raindrops" / "To Headlights": These two poems were, due to my own oversight, misprinted in the original edition of *The Martyr, the Grizzly, the Gold*. The text of "To Raindrops" was mistakenly given the title "To Headlights," and the text of "To Headlights" was left out entirely.

This misprint was first corrected in the 2017 digital chapbook edition of *Exalt!*.

Four Counties was one of my first poems ever published, but has never been collected until now. It was included in early drafts of *The Martyr, the Grizzly, the Gold*, but was ultimately left out due to its length and the formal and stylistic differences to the other poems in the collection. The four counties mentioned in the poem titles are counties in central California (Ventura and San Luis Obispo) and southern California (Riverside and Los Angeles).

About the Author

Timothy E. G. Bartel is a poet and professor from California. He holds an MFA in Poetry from Seattle Pacific University and a PhD in Theology, Imagination, and Arts from University of St. Andrews. Timothy's poems, translations, and essays have been published widely, including in *Christianity and Literature, First Things, The Hopkins Review, Notes & Queries, Saint Katherine Review,* and *Windhover.* Timothy's books include *The Martyr, the Grizzly, the Gold* (Damascene Press, 2012), *Arroyos: Sijo and other Poems* (Mariscat Press, 2015), *Aflame but Unconsumed: Poems* (Kelsay Books, 2019), and *Glimpses of Her Father's Glory: Deification and Divine Light in Longfellow's "Evangeline"* (Wipf & Stock, 2019). In 2012, alongside Jonathan A. Diaz, Timothy founded the *Californios Review*, a digital periodical which published new creative writing by emerging West Coast writers. Timothy currently edits the Californios Chapbook Series and serves as Professor of Great Texts and Writing at Saint Constantine College.

www.ingramcontent.com/pod-product-compliance
Lightning Source LLC
Chambersburg PA
CBHW030300100526
44590CB00012B/465